Other books by Marilyn Hacker

GOING BACK
TO THE
R I V E R

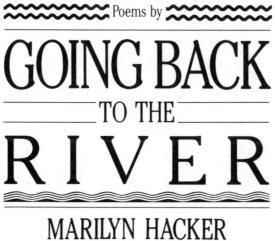

~~~~~~ Poems by ~~~~~~

GOING BACK
TO THE
R I V E R

MARILYN HACKER

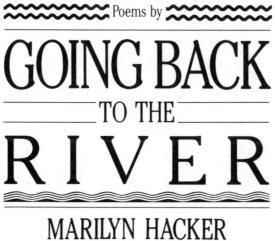 Random House New York

All rights reserved under International and Pan-American Copyright
Conventions. Published in the United States by Random House, Inc.,
New York, and simultaneously in Canada by Random House of
Canada Limited, Toronto.

Library of Congress Cataloging-in-Publication Data
Hacker, Marilyn.
Going back to the river : poems / by Marilyn Hacker.
p. cm.
ISBN 0-394-58271-3
I. Title
PS3558.A28G86   1990
811'.54-dc20   89-28290
                                                       CIP

Acknowledgment is gratefully given to the following periodicals,
in which many of the poems in this volume originally appeared:
*Ambit, Boulevard, Christopher Street, City Lights Review, Conditions,
Fiction International, The Graham House Review, Manhattan Poetry
Review, New Letters, The New York Quarterly, Open Places, The Paris
Review, Prairie Schooner, River Styx, Rubicon, The Yale
Review*.

"Nights of 1962: The River Merchant's Wife," "Nights of 1964–1966:
The Old Reliable," "Elevens," and "Days of 1944: Three Friends"
were originally published in *Grand Street.*

"Late August," "Cultural Exchange," and "For K.J., Leaving and
Coming Back" were originally published in *Ploughshares.*

"April Interval I" was originally published in *Poetry.*

"Then" and "Letter from Goose Creek: April" were originally
published in *Yellow Silk.*

"Letter from Goose Creek: April" received the Robert H. Winner
Memorial Award of the Poetry Society of America in 1987.
"Against Silence" received a Pushcart Prize in 1989 and was published
in the *Pushcart Prize Anthology XIV.*
"Two Cities" received the Robert H. Winner Memorial Award of the
Poetry Society of America in 1989.

Grateful acknowledgment is made to the following for permission to
reprint previously published material: STEPHEN BISHOP MUSIC
PUBLISHING COMPANY AND CPP/BELWIN, INC.: Excerpt from song
lyrics "Separate Lives" by Stephen Bishop. Copyright © 1985 by
Stephen Bishop Publishing Company, Hidden Pun Music, Inc., and
Gold Horizon Music Corporation (BMI). International Copyright
secured. Made in USA. All right reserved. Used by permission. TOM
DISCH AND THE JOHNS HOPKINS UNIVERSITY PRESS: Excerpts from
"Working on a Tan" from *Yes, Let's . . . New and Selected Poems* by
Tom Disch (The Johns Hopkins University Press, 1989). Reprinted by
permission of Tom Disch and The Johns Hopkins University Press.

Manufactured in the United States of America
24689753
First Edition

For K. J.,
for years and seasons,
nights and days

～～～ Contents ～～～

AGAINST SILENCE

TWO CITIES

TWO CITIES

I

The streetlights bent
the sleet streams as I went
up the deserted Rue des Deux-Ponts,

the only one
except two boy drunks on
the steep slope of Rue Cardinal-Lemoine.

I took the sharp
turn toward the Place de la Contrescarpe.
Firelight shimmered in the rain. A group

of tramps, five men,
two women, warmed their hands
over an open fire in an oil-drum.

Rain beat down hard.
A bear-man with a beard
passed the glistening bottle of *pinard*

to an old one,
who tipped it. Her red cheeks shone
like a child's, come in from the sun.

I had both your
keys for the Rue Tournefort,
and my own, for back across the river.

It cleared my head
when I walked from desk to bed,
rive droite, rive gauche, the distance I needed.

That "worst winter
in decades," crossing the center
of Paris, I was the inventor

of my own life,
an old plane tree in new leaf,
a young woman almost forty-five.

II

When I was sick
I stayed under the thick
couch cover, with the electric

fire on three bars,
drapes pulled to muffle cars
and buses passing, a sweatshirt (yours)

keeping my arms
warm while I read. A rainstorm
chewed on last night's snow; a fire alarm

ripped the thick air
outside, not my interior
weather. Earl Grey with milk. Dusk fell at four-

thirty. Neighbors
pulling shopping carts upstairs
stopped with the ninety-year-old next door

eager to un-
latch for the Rue Saint-Antoine
gossip with her evening bread and wine.

Tiny, bird-boned,
daily she'd done her own
errands, seven decades living alone,

until she slipped
on iced stairs and cracked her hip.
She wants the food less than the gossip.

Hands round my cup,
I thought how you'd come up-
stairs too in three hours. We'd cut bread, ladle soup,

pour wine, refill
the glasses for my cold, your chilled
hands, lie down to sleep together until

her radio
at six A.M. let us know
the night had come and gone next door also.

III

The carrot-top
above the Mom-and-Pop
hardware shook out her dust mop,

a cigarette
in her mouth. Three years, I'd yet
to see her dressed. She slapped a small carpet

on the worked rail,
square in a square nightshirt. The trail
of dust and ashes floated past the mail

truck, sun-yellow,
leg-up on the curb, pillowed
on grimy snow. In the window below,

a gray woman
checked what the shoppers had on
and buttoned up a black cardigan.

Two boys, short pants,
school satchels on their backs, danced
with cold at the bus stop, rubbing their hands.

In the dormer
window of the former
maid's room, chinked rags kept somebody warmer.

A flock of gray
clouds at roof-peak skirled away.
The blue banner of a windy day

unfurled while I
poured a fresh cup of coffee
laced with hot milk, and sat and watched it fly.

IV

Nine months later,
on a terrace with my daughter,
eating *moules,* we saw the blue-jeaned waiter

abruptly turn
his gorgeous Euro-African
profile toward upper Broadway, where a young,

or not young, blonde
cursed out the night around
her, and someone who'd knocked her down.

Drunk? Crack? Her mind?
She slashed in front, behind
herself with a slim cane. "I think she's blind!"

Iva whispered
as the woman disappeared
past the balcony. As if she'd heard,

she turned, came back,
cheeks slack, gray anorak
in September, brandishing her stick.

She lunged with it
and raked the table opposite
us. Plates crashed, glass shattered. "Damn you, you shit!"

addressed to no
one specific. When you know
the words so well, they're not vivid argot,

only despair,
as the beautiful waiter
vaulted the rail, pinioned her there

till the cop van
came. The couple got free wine
at a fresh table while the floor was cleaned.

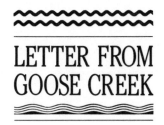

LETTER FROM
GOOSE CREEK

NIGHTS OF 1962:
THE RIVER MERCHANT'S WIFE

—for Carol Lee Hane

Emigrée from the Bronx, a married child
hit the ghetto-turned-barrio, making wild
conjectures and conjunctions, making wrong
turns on lyrics of country-and-western songs.
Moondark to dawn, loud streets were not-quite-scary
footnotes in a nocturnal dictionary
of argot softer on my ears than known
four-walled cadenzas to: the night alone,
the day on fire. (My age, the boss boy knew.)
From Avenue C west to Sixth Avenue
and Eighth Street, I'd aim for the all-night Whelan's,
eat solo ham and eggs. The night sky paled, sands
into the river's timer. One more day:
jeans switched for dark dress, tight shoes, the subway
to work at Altman's. Five months short of twenty,
I knocked back whatever the river sent. He
was gone two days; might bring back, on the third,
some kind of night music I'd never heard:
Sonny the burglar, paunched with breakfast beers;
olive-skinned Simon, who made fake Vermeers;
the cardsharp who worked club cars down the coast;
Carol, stone butch, who'd booked Chip's group, was host,
bouncer, bookkeeper, and night manager
of a folk club. The night she spotted her
sometime girlfriend naked in my red chalk
drawings taped to the john wall, we had a talk
about how she bridged night's work and day's work,
a dude till dawn, a nine-to-five file clerk

in heels and hose. Some grass: she demonstrated
her butch walk, girl walk, paced, like a five-gaited
horse, the splintered floor, miming her cross-
over from flunky to three A.M. yard boss.
Fox-faced in burnt sienna, the judge's daughter
ignored us. Was it Carol who had bought her
the watch she left on, posing, to keep time?
I learned the lesson as a paradigm
of living day-life, night-life, Janus-faced.
Why didn't Carol, older, have her own place?
Where did she sleep the nights she didn't crash
on our spare mattress at East Fifth Street? Cash
she stored in the front pocket of her drip-
dry chinos, which she slept on, laid out under
the mattress for their knife-edge. Who, I wondered,
did she sleep *with*, now? She'd told things to Chip
she wouldn't tell me, who'd only (she'd guess) botched
stoned fumblings while somebody's boyfriend watched.
I knew the boys' bars—did she go to one
for girls? I dawdled nights on the question.
Two weeks later: what did they make of me
on a barstool at the Sea Colony
in a paint-splattered Black Watch shirt, old khak-
i work pants, one long braid straight down my back,
chain-smoking Camels, making my second Bud
last? I sipped it as slowly as I could,
looking around me surreptitiously.
Boys' bars had dance floors. Puerto Rican queens
in mohair sweaters, who'd worked up routines
in kitchens, line-danced to "No Milk Today,"
"From a Jack to a Queen," "Walk Like a Man,"
too cool to giggle at the *double enten-*

dres, cruising without seeming to cruise.
No one was dancing here. Women in twos,
each suit-and-tie paired with a plunge-necked sheath,
held hands at tiny tables, closed. Bad teeth
and Brooklyn accents, nineteen-year-old snob
thought, in the wrong outfit for either job
—and how invade with chat hermetically
sealed couples? Somebody romantically
forty-plus, foreign, solitary, face
defined by facing danger, in this place
for R & R, who'd like my mind, whose bed,
dovetailed by bookshelves, was four blocks away . . .
Seduction by the French Department head
to whom I owed a paper on Genet
was what I had in mind, and I assumed
she'd know how to proceed beyond the full-
face closeup kiss on which my mind's lens zoomed
in, blanked out. I should have followed Carol
on her night off. She knew the regulars,
I guessed. I couldn't sit on a barstool
reading, till closing. Chip had adventures;
I, it seemed, had trepidations. Full
of them, I got down the rest of my beer
and turned tail, out the door into the night
streets, which aroused just reasonable fear.
I lengthened my strides streetlight to streetlight,
in no hurry to regain the empty
conjugal crash pad and wait out the dregs
of the dark. I was, I told myself, hungry
enough to hit Whelan's for ham and eggs.

APRIL INTERVAL

Wherever I surface I reinvent
some version of the Daily Walk to Town:
two miles rewarded with an hour's browse round
the market square or its equivalent:
a yard sale off the Dyer County Road,
Rua Visconde de Pirajá.
Company is unwanted as a car.
I have, I've found, an operative code.
Perhaps, at forty, I'm escaping Nurse
Conscience to look for Mother in the shops;
perhaps irregularities, slow stops,
burst-starts of footfall echo feats of verse.
Perhaps it's just that I procrastinate
incorrigibly, as I've always done,
justified by a footpath splashed with sun.
Precipitation is precipitate.
Now I'm an orphaned spinster with a home
where spoils of these diurnal expeditions
can be displayed in prominent positions.
I'll hang this crazy quilt in the front room,
its unembarrassedly polychrome
velvet rhomboids and uneven satin
patches lined with fancywork, no pattern
twice. She painted flowers and leaves on some

a hundred years ago. I know it's "she."
"The life," at my age, will only be "sweet"
as I make it. I can't guarantee
myself a Boston marriage or more money,
but I can be outdoors and on my feet
as long as I'm still sound, and it's still sunny.

LITERARY INITIATION c. 1960

—for Sharon Olds

Expansively to his bar-entourage,
the poet said, "What I need tonight
is a skirt!" The schoolgirl thought, "Poor man"—
and swiped her Harvard cousin's beer (a fan,
he'd brought her there as bait, or camouflage),
—"he's a genius, but he's a transvestite!"

SELF

I did it
differently:
moistened two
fingers in my mouth,
touched
with curiosity,
desire, what I'd
squeezed spasms from before
to get to sleep.
As I would touch an
other's
fullness, blood-ripe
(I was from dreaming
her pleasure
pleasuring
me), I felt
myself, touched
what she would touch me
to, what I
treasured (unexamined),
and ignored.
Velvety, floriform
animal breathes
body-wet like a parched
snail, water;
still, dry,
slicked to a bearing
rolls in place

rooted
where I learned to love
entering; am entered.
Pleasure connects
those parts, nerves whose duty is delight:
a self-contained utopian
dialogue on the beautiful: quin-
tessentially human.

SATURDAY NIGHT BILE

Multiple
relationships? I like waking up
mornings in a row
doing it
the fifth time in two days.
Somebody
always sounds like
a dentist advocating
root canal. Multiple
relationships: dates
to meet, tentative as teenagers.
Perennial
courtship. I don't like
courtship; its pleasures are intense
but febrile. I like kitchen pleasures:
familiar eggbeater,
third cup of coffee,
not
cringing when the phone rings.
Three in one bed:
hard to work it, worth it
when it works. One in three beds:
twelve potential animosities,
Saturday night bile.

RIPOSTE

(I never could
Figure out how anyone can justify poetry
As a full-time job. How do they get through
The day at MacDowell—filling out
Applications for the next free lunch?)
—TOM DISCH: "Working on a Tan"

Dear Tom,

      When my next volume (granted: slender)
is granted an advance of more than two
thou, perhaps I'll scorn all grants and spend a
couple of them on summer rent, like you,

in the right Hampton with the novelists
who swap Hollywood options with bravado.
Their *au pairs* hoard handwritten shopping-lists;
their word-processors go with them to Yaddo

where novelists are still *persona grata,*
nor do their royalties or last advance
cause the *per diem* charge to rise *pro rata.*
I'd ever so much rather be in France

and not have to eat dinner at six-thirty
with frozen carrots and Kraft's French (*sic*) Dressing.
But potshotting "free-lunch" is playing dirty;
successful applicants should count their blessings.

I wouldn't want the kitchen staff to brand me
an ingrate who will bite the hand that feeds me

if I am going to eat the food they hand me
—and they're in the minority that reads me.

Is poetry a full-time occupation?
Practitioners have spliced it with exciting
alternative careers in transportation
—drive cabs, that is—or teach Creative Writing

or First-Year French or Freshman Composition,
translate, wait tables, sell insurance, edit.
If "poet" 's written where it says: PROFESSION:
American Express extends no credit.

And you see no excuse for poets' lives
because we're paid so mingily; that's it?
I think of "unemployed" mothers, housewives
whose work was judged equivalent to shit-

shoveling on Frank Perdue's chicken farm
by gents who calibrate Job Equity.
All that they are today they owe to Mom!
Do novelists owe shit to poetry?

SF writer snipes poets on the pages
of *Poetry*: that's also aiming low,
though nowhere near as low as poets' wages.
At fifty cents a line, where would *you* go?

And fifty cents a line's exemplary!
Measure it to your last *Playboy* short-short
and you might find an artists' colony
a perfectly respectable resort.

THE LAST APRIL INTERVAL

Eight o'clock, nine o'clock,
Coffee and oranges,
"Do you want eggs?" for the
Twenty-fifth time.
(*Orange* is singular.)
"No, I want caviar,
Onions, black bread, and a
Vodka and lime."

Nine o'clock, ten o'clock,
Leftover hangover,
Stare at the typewriter,
Epithets fail.
Light up, break training,
It's (anyway) raining,
Extinguish the cigarette,
See if there's mail.

Twelve o'clock, one o'clock,
Butterscotch Lifesavers,
Thermos of coffee that's
Tepid and black.
I know my lunch will be
Carrots and celery,
Carrots alone in a
Brown-paper sack.

Three o'clock, four o'clock,
Books on the lamp-table,
Smell on my fingers of
Coal-tar shampoo.
Wash out some underwear
(no more clean socks), prepare
For a long measure of
Nothing to do.

Five o'clock, six o'clock,
Something unthinkable—
What if the *food* is as
Bad as last night's?
Hogs in their pens may en-
Dure such Dickensian
Swill, but some women have
Strange appetites.

Eight o'clock, nine o'clock,
Back from the dining room.
Some of the Fellows are
Driving to town.
I don't want beer; I feel
Visibly queer. (A meal
I cooked at home would be
Just getting down.)

Nine o'clock, ten o'clock,
Nuns singing evensong,
Sisters in scapulars

Sway alongside.
I think they ought to try
Horae Canonicae
Here to keep renegade
Souls occupied.

LATE AUGUST LETTER

—for Eavan Boland

Dear Eavan,
Just yesterday afternoon
in my notebook I'd written
your letter on my wish list
for August. On Assumption

your round hand
was under the Eire stamp and
salmon-turquoise Airmail band
on the mail table. Sprung from
the boredom of boarders' bland

school dinners
where the chosen word-spinners,
shape-makers mind their manners,
I felt like a local track
maverick who'd picked winners.

On the free-
way outside the colony
mill rugose beef-bloat poly-
acrylic American
racing fans. From family

armored cars
they haul flattened web lawn chairs,
inevitable coolers
of beer they truck through the dust
for the thirst they'll rouse with cheers.

Half-past ten,
the streets are silent again.
No women gossip, no men
play cards. From each house I walk
past glares chalk television-

light: canned noise
recorded sometime/where else.
No children are making noise.
Through the black trees, one dimmed star.
From their car, out-of-town boys,

holiday-
drunk, cruise for something to lay.
(Ten bars: one is "sort of gay.")
I cross; they drive on, no hass-
le, I pass—passed as a boy?

Dawn: racecourse
misted, glimpsed totemic horse
shapes incarnate grace's force.
One leans on his girl groom's knee
being refreshed with a hose.

Children ex-
ercise them mornings at six.
She, arrowed from her mount's neck's
thundering into the sky.
I walk by, cracking dry sticks

underfoot
in the hoofprinted mud, out
before coffee—none until eight!
I measure distance enough
to stave off my caffeine fit.

Breakfast's on
in the art-nouveau mansion
turned, in one generation,
hothouse for artists' labors.
My neighbor's Nigerian—

he's "the one."
Whitefolk are almost legion
(and childed single women).
One black woman novelist
left the rest to eat alone

every day
in West House. Her grocery
bags were tagged in the pantry.
Weeks, and I never met her.
(Another woman told me.)

I'm the queer
apple in the barrel here.
A playwright-novelist pair
may be indulging in a
Claudine à l'école affair—

but I'm just
as contented to be chaste,
though quite cognizant that last
statement may appear to be
irony by April first.

In Ireland
—where the midsummer high ground
of your talk excited wan-
derlust in me to be—how
are you now, what work's at hand?

I haven't
said, but I do imagine
the peaks of conversation
we might scale if I were there,
or you nearby, dear Eavan.

THEN

I was due home at seven, and you were
staying downtown. We shared a premature
glass of white wine.
               "I'll walk you downstairs."
                        "Sure."
Out on the dim landing, you pushed the door
shut behind us, one hand on the small
of my back, then pushed me back against the wall
hung with winter coats. I almost slipped
in the half-dark; half-gasped as you unzipped
my pants and tugged them down, silencing my
exclamation with your tongue, your thigh
opening mine. I grabbed your ass with one
hand, hair with the other. You began
stroking my belly, but I pulled you close
against me, covering what you'd exposed.
You whispered, "Should I get down on my knees
and lick you?"
            "No, with your hand, like that, there, please!"
Mouth on your mouth, I rode you, barely stand-
ing up, or standing it. You moved your hand
past where I put it, through the parting, wet
for you already, spread me, and I let
you deep in, while your lips went soft beneath
my mouth, and I tasted salt behind your teeth.
Your fingers brought the juices down around
what swelled into your palm, until you found
where it would come from. Inches of my bare

skin burned against your jeans. Into your hair
I pleaded, "Let me," but you wouldn't; pulled
a centimeter back, instead. The chill
air on my skin pulsed through me like a smack,
and, for a breath, I let my head fall back
against the linen sleeves and woolen folds,
then drew you onto me, so I could hold
myself up to your kisses, while you took
me, out and in, with your whole hand. I shook,
off balance, needed it, you, just there. I
thrust up against you. Then my inner thigh
muscles convulsed, and I bore down on you,
wrenching out "Now!" as heat arrowed into
the place you had me, till I couldn't stop
it coming, crushed against you, half on top
of you, or you on me, breathed through your lips
a huge, collapsing sigh. Arms around my hips,
holding my ass, you kissed me as I hung
on your shoulders, prodded my hair back with your tongue.
You covered me till I recovered my
balance, and my butt, to say, "Good-bye."
"Call you later."

                   "Ummm." Buttoned, I pushed
away, blinking, stepped back. "I've got to rush,"
and watched my footing down three rickety
flights toward twilight traffic in Chelsea.

TORCH

Pillar of sequins in a Saturday-
night club, or did she bob in Alice Faye
Peter Pan collar to the microphone,
cradle it, while she mooned at him, and croon
fifties kitsch, but clean as a plain gold ring?
He liked to hear her sing. She liked to sing.
Twenty-seven to his forty-four,
ex-cashier and rag-trade entrepreneur,
both smoked like gangsters, liked good Scotch, closed bars.
So does their daughter, who keeps three guitars
for late-night chord changes in a dim room,
and has stood up behind a podium.
Why did the red-headed torch singer quit
the spotlight, spouse, their child? It doesn't fit.
However she puts pieces together,
all she has left is the one who left her
fair hair, a Celtic temper, a torch song
and a walk-out. She also started young.

COUNTRY & WESTERN

She will never know I cried for her
in a motel outside Memphis, far
west as you go in the East. By TV light
—Clark Gable hunted the last mustangs down
while Marilyn Monroe wept in the pickup—
Julie smoked in bed, restless, a headache

coming on, as my two-day headache
receded, and the rain steamed dry. In her
Toyota, we'd come a thousand miles. She'd pick up
her bloke in Phoenix, come from Nice, a far
cry from where she'd packed the car: a down
vest for the Rockies, Coleman stove, flashlight,

tent, lantern, three months' books. I traveled light,
along for a week's driving, a headach-
y novice. At the river, rain sluiced down
the windshield. Julie drank Wild Turkey from her
plastic flask. Teenagers in a pickup
tossed beer cans, almost visible, as far

as the riverbank erased by rain. We'd fore-
cast storms: no wet camping. When torrents light-
ened up, we struck the tent. I'd have tried to pick up
the blond girl Ranger, but my headache
throbbed: nothing else could. While I talked to her
I hurt. We thought she thought she had us down

as lovers when she said which motel down
the road would have us: Northern women, for-
eigners. She'd *one* red fingernail; beneath her
Hawaiian shirt, a gold cross. In the last light
we drove off, checked in. I left my headache
in the Montana Bar. Steaks, beer: when I pick up

a glass, a fork, I know my mood will pick up
too, and it did, till, later, I lay down
on that square hired bed. She was in my head: ache
in a severed part a thousand miles weren't far
enough to salve. She'd pick that film, her Lite
beside the bed. Not Julie, not the Ranger: her

hand not far from her crotch, blond head near my head, ach-
ing back I'd pound; she'd pick up, then put down
the beer . . . I doused the light. I cried for her.

COUNTRY & WESTERN II

It looks like we are the Last Unmarried
Women in Tucson. We talk about food,
drinking, and mountains. They talk about babies.
We're going to have to go outside to smoke.
Is there any more bourbon in the car?
It's too early to want to go to bed

in sleeping bags *indoors.* Fun in bed
in Tucson happens after you get married
—why every teenager has got a car.
As your friend peeled and chopped, we talked about food
we'd cooked at campsites: *molé con* charcoal smoke
for two nights running. She talked about babies

and I remembered talking about babies
incessantly, when I had one, in bed
in a basket under my desk. I'd smoke,
swill coffee, and discuss her. I stayed married
for nine months after that. We talk about food
in the morning, while you waltz the car

around the mall, for space next to a car
bigger enough to vouchsafe shade (a BABY's
ON BOARD, decals announce). We talk about food
on down the Giant's twelve aisles, each one a Bed
of Procrustes. Do you *want* to get married,
and why? There's fire, but you've had all that smoke

in your eyes before. If I could smoke
dope without crashing, I'd say, let's take the car
up one of your mountains. Sunset married
to sky, we'd gaze, get high. If your friend's baby-
sitter showed up, she'd come too—but her bed-
and-board-mate would get home and want his food.

O, even gorged with cheap Mexican food,
the counterculture, rounding forty (smoke
defiantly, hint an unlicensed bed
or two, have drinking buddies now incar-
cerated), still had curfews: home to babies.
"A toast, first, to these two, who just got married!"

(The rest, like me, married when they were babies.)
Before bedtime, we'll toast your yellow car,
smoke while we watch the stars, and talk about food.

FROM ORIENT POINT

The art of living isn't hard to muster:
Enjoy the hour, not what it might portend.
When someone makes you promises, don't trust her

unless they're in the here and now, and just her
willing largesse free-handed to a friend.
The art of living isn't hard to muster:

groom the old dog, her coat gets back its luster;
take brisk walks so you're hungry at the end.
When someone makes you promises, don't trust her

to know she can afford what they will cost her
to keep until they're kept. Till then, pretend
the art of living isn't hard to muster.

Cooking, eating and drinking are a cluster
of pleasures. Next time, don't go round the bend
when someone makes you promises. Don't trust her

past where you'd trust yourself, and don't adjust her
words to mean more to you than she'd intend.
The art of living isn't hard to muster.

You never had her, so you haven't lost her
like spare house keys. Whatever *she* opens,
when someone makes you promises, don't. Trust your
art; go on living: that's not hard to muster.

LETTER FROM GOOSE CREEK: APRIL

—for K. J.

We're both in Greenville, but a state apart.
About the time you were due to arrive,
I was helping Julie stack wood for the stove.
There was frost last night. When we had to start
the fire up, I remembered you, me, and the dog
sprawled out on the brown-and-gold rag rug
as you wedged twigs and kindling till the log
caught; then you and I kindled from a hug
while the fire blazed, from slow afternoon's talking.
Bright afternoon here now, through which I drove
two-lanes at a journeyman's fifty-five
thirty miles to Goose Creek from the K-Mart
—smooth starts at traffic lights are still the worst part.
What changes nothing changes everything.

There are no detours circumventing grief.
The spare-room pillow's littered with the "Tracks
Of My Tears" again. I came unstuck
at dawn when gray light off-printed oak-leaf
shapes, vague as clouds before; and then, my eyes
hopelessly open, I pulled last night's clothes
back on. Outside the window, three outsize
woodpeckers in the feeder and a rose-
breasted she-cardinal were bickering
while I rattled round Julie's kitchen, look-
ing for the coffeepot. The falling back's
inevitable. I know you know brief
descents yourself. Juice, coffee, and relief.
What changes nothing changes everything.

You were the friend who got me through the night
I packed her things. It was a few nights after,
when, stuck on upper Broadway in your car
with postal sacks you'd ferried me to get,
"Was I a good friend, or an inadequate
lover?" you asked, about our friend, who'd died
with you, months vigilant by her bedside,
years warily defining why and what
you couldn't. Then the wind had you, raging
your mourning across a continent we were
sometimes conjoined by, like the curiouser
fossils. From my stratum, trilobite
dislodged, bordering yours, I did what might
have changed nothing, or changes everything.

Cold rain sheeted the Long Island Expressway
the Ides of March, commuters on our necks.
We were, I noticed, talking about sex
in a half-gossip, half "I should confess . . . " way.
I know I thought, "I wonder where this gets
us, in the rain, stuck indoors on our butts
days, at the edge of nowhere?" I said, "Let's,"
eventually. Trust me: it took guts
even in the dark, and in the dark, and in the morning,
a new diplomacy to hold the checks
and balances of night, which brought the next
night's badges of courage. I undressed, lay
down with you, until our hands found the best way,
changing nothing, of changing everything.

There isn't question of an instant replay.
The past hasn't sufficiently gone past
for that to be in either's interest.
Still, in the night beside you, I could sleep; stay
sane through a blighted anniversary
walking beside the water in daylight.
I didn't think of her when you touched me,
though she brought my insomnia last night
and in the live oaks is a lingering
absence. While you're being a houseguest
inland, I try, near the Atlantic coast,
something you taught me well enough to keep—see
that something in you touched something in me deeply.
What changes nothing changes everything.

How many states and interstates and cities
will find us, our miles and our trajectories
between us, both maneuvering strange keys
to borrowed rooms? Some faculty committees
will host me, while your wanderlust hosts you
from friend to friend, vistas you never saw
before, to mornings with completely new
prospects, suggesting that you stay or go
on: suddenly an interesting
itinerary on the map of raw
absence. If you weren't young till now,
now's the time. Reading the highways
between the lines, you're geared, you're gone. The key's
what changes. Nothing changes everything.

This morning I sent you a postcard of
East Carolina University.
You need to learn disponibility.
I yearn to feel I'm central where I love.
That's a difference. Friendships survive, can thrive
on differences. Yours and mine has. Julie and I've
lived ours. A beach walk followed a midday drive.
Sheltered by boulders, with the dog, beside
the Sound in sunlight, you and I made spring
welcome. Because we did, it is today
welcome still, on the live oak trail, while Julie
reads Cather on a deck chair in the cove.
What's possible is possible: enough
that change is: that one thing changes everything.

NIGHTS OF 1964–1966:
THE OLD RELIABLE

—for Lewis Ellingham

The laughing soldiers fought to their defeat
—JAMES FENTON: "In a Notebook"

White decorators interested in Art,
Black file clerks with theatrical ambitions,
kids making pharmaceutical revisions
in journals Comp. instructors urged they start,
the part-Cherokee teenage genius (maybe),
the secretary who hung out with fairies,
the copywriter wanting to know, where is
my husband? the soprano with the baby,
all drank draught beer or lethal sweet Manhattans
or improvised concoctions with tequila
in summer when, from Third Street, we could feel a
night breeze waft in whose fragrances were Latin.
The place was run by Polish refugees:
squat Margie, gaunt Speedy (whose sobriquet
transliterated what?). He'd brought his play
from Łódź. After a while, we guessed Margie's
illiteracy was why *he* cashed checks
and *she* perched near the threshold to ban pros,
the underage, the fugitive, and those
arrayed impertinently to their sex.
The bar was talk and cruising; in the back
room, we danced: Martha and the Vandellas,
Smokey and the Miracles, while sellers

and buyers changed crisp tens for smoke and smack.
Some came in after work, some after supper,
plumage replenished to meet who knew who.
Behind the bar, Margie dished up beef stew.
On weeknights, you could always find an upper
to speed you to your desk, and drink till four.
Loosened by booze, we drifted, on the ripples
of Motown, home in new couples, or triples,
were back at dusk, with ID's, at the door.
Bill was my roommate, Russell drank with me,
although they were a dozen years my seniors.
I walked off with the eighteen-year-old genius
—an Older Woman, barely twenty-three.
Link was new as Rimbaud, and better looking,
North Beach bar *paideon* of doomed Jack Spicer,
like Russell, our two-meter artificer,
a Corvo whose *ecclesia* was cooking.
Bill and Russell were painters. Bill had been
a monk in Kyoto. Stoned, we sketched together,
till he discovered poppers and black leather
and Zen consented to new discipline.
We shared my Sixth Street flat with a morose
cat, an arch cat, and pot plants we pruned daily.
His boyfriend had left him for an Israeli
dancer; my husband was on Mykonos.
Russell loved Harold who was Black and bad,
and lavished on him dinners "meant for men"
like Escoffier and Brillat-Savarin.
Staunch blond Dora made rice. When she had
tucked in the twins, six flights of tenement
stairs they'd descend, elevenish, and stroll
down Third Street, desultory night patrol

gone mauve and green under the virulent
streetlights, to the bar, where Bill and I
(if we'd not come to dinner), Link, and Lew,
and Betty had already had a few.
One sweat-soaked night in pitiless July,
wedged on booth-benches of cracked Naugahyde,
we planned a literary magazine
where North Beach met the Lower East Side Scene.
We could have titled it *When Worlds Collide.*
Dora was gone, "In case the children wake up."
Link lightly had decamped with someone else
(the German engineer? Or was he Bill's?).
Russell's stooped *vale* brushed my absent makeup.
Armed children spared us home, our good-night hugs
laissez-passer. We railed against the war.
Soon, some of us bussed south with SNCC and CORE.
Soon, some of us got busted dealing drugs.
The file clerks took exams and forged ahead.
The decorators' kitchens blazed persimmon.
The secretary started kissing women,
and so did I, and my three friends are dead.

ELEVENS

There is one story and one story only
—ROBERT GRAVES: "To Juan at the Winter Solstice"

James A. Wright, my difficult older brother,
I'm in an airplane over your Ohio.
Twice a week, there and back, I make this journey
to Cincinnati.

You are six books I own and two I borrowed.
I'm the songs about the drunk on the runway
and leaving your lover for the airport, first
thing in the morning.

You were fifty-two when you died of cancer
of the tongue, apologist for the lonely
girls who were happened to near some bleak water.
Tell me about it.

When my father died young, my mother lost it.
I am only three years younger than he was.
The older brother and the younger brother
that I never had

died young, in foreign cities, uncomforted.
Does anybody not die uncomforted?
My friend Sonny had her lovers around her
and she died also.

Half drunk on sunlight in my second country,
I yearned through six-line stanzas I learned from you.
You spent January of your last winter
up on that mountain.

I love a boy who died and a girl who left.
I love a brother who is a grown woman.
I love your eight books. I hate the ending.
I never knew you.

You knew a lot about airports and rivers
and a girl who went away in October.
Fathers, brothers and sisters die of cancer:
still, we are strangers.

You are the lonely gathering of rivers
below the plane that left you in Ohio;
you are the fog of language on Manhattan
where it's descending.

MARKET DAY

MARKET DAY

Quand la vie est dure, les dur(e)s vont au marché.

Today is the *jour de marché*
downhill from Nullepart-sur-Colline.
In white voile for the heat of the day,
the secondhand Benetton jeans,

downhill from Nullepart-sur-Colline,
I take the goatpath through the woods.
The secondhand Benetton jeans
ward off horseflies and gnats, as they should.

I take the goatpath through the woods
till the narrow *ruelles* to the square
ward off horseflies and gnats. As they should,
with baskets, the *bonnes ménagères*

till the narrow *ruelles* to the square,
precede me to cherries and bread.
With baskets, the *bonnes ménagères*
are *aïeules,* behind and ahead.

Precede me to cherries and bread
in communion you shared before I did.
Our *aïeules* behind and ahead,
your grandmothers, students, were guided

in communion you shared before I did,
annealing the task to the leisure.
Your grandmothers' students were guided:
"woman's work" may include woman's pleasure.

Annealing the task to the leisure,
I pick a live trout for my dinner.
Woman's work may include woman's pleasure—
if I were a little bit thinner.

I pick a live trout for my dinner
with a few leaves of wintergreen *blettes*.
If I were a little bit thinner,
what delicious confections I'd get:

with a few leaves of wintergreen *blettes*
and cheese, are made heavenly pies.
What delicious confections I'd get
at the *fripes,* if I'd shave down one size!

(But the cheese! and the heavenly pies!)
I can figure out all the Swiss labels
at the *fripes,* if I shave down one size
from French in the heaps on the tables.

I can figure out all the Swiss labels,
but the Languedoc twang's pretty far
from French. In the heaps on the tables,
buried under the *polyestère*

(but the Languedoc twang's pretty far
down in) are mauve silk and beige cotton.
Buried under the *polyestère,*
surpassing the treasures I've gotten

down in, are mauve silk and beige cotton
for the lives that I wish that I led.
Surpassing the treasures I've gotten
in my time, there's a hoard in my head.

For the lives that I wish that I led
have these garments, these victuals as staples.
In my time, there's a hoard in my head
to be laid out on college-ruled paper.

Have these garments, these victuals, as staples
the transformative substance required
to be laid out on college-ruled paper
like a loaf brushed with gold for the fire?

The transformative substance required:
a coin in the hand of the maker.
Like a loaf? Brushed with gold from the fire,
ranked according to size by the bakers.

"A coin in the hand of the maker!"
The Romany weaver of baskets,
ranked according to size by the baker's
snacking biscuits, pursues me to ask it.

The Romany weaver of baskets
—while her daughters tend wares as they laugh,
snacking biscuits—pursues me to ask: "It's
made to last! Will you take it for half?"

While her daughters tend wares, as they laugh,
one counts change, one is plaiting new reeds,
made to last. "Will you take it for half?"
Now it's here, filled with things that I need.

One counts change, one is plaiting new reeds,
in white voile for the heat of the day.
Now it's here, filled with things that I need:
today is the *jour de marché.*

AFTER ASSUMPTION

Yesterday, closed shops,
ribboned cake-boxes, candied
fruits: She Is Risen.

Moment by moment
clouds shift, the weather changes.
Wind stirs my coffee.

Table: nine gray planks
soaked through in a midnight storm,
sun-dried before noon.

Like a scythe chopping,
crickets chirrup. The back door
bangs shut and open.

Blackberries ripen
in the scrub bushes again:
rump half of August.

Silence, now. Crickets
only chitter in sunshine.
The sun is hidden.

More rain comes blowing
north over the coastal hills;
fog shrouds the mountains.

LATE AUGUST

The weather is changing. The mountainous temperate cli-
   mate
edges toward autumn.
There's a crowded sound in the rattling leaves of the fig tree
and I think of cities,
though the second fruit, ovarian, purple, splitting to scarlet
is ready for picking.
The brambles hedging pink villas banked up from the road-
   way
burgeon with berries
ripening black, seeded, sweet, which the French don't
   bother to gather,
but sometimes I do,
taking an extra plastic bag in my back pocket, coming
up from the market.
I'm less often tempted to strip off my shirt in the morning
at work on the terrace.
The bedsheets are grimy and wrinkled, but why should we
   haul
to the costly laundry
what we'd need for a couple of days? All our conversations
touch on departure.

ALBA NEAR IMPRUNETA

They wake to January light
a cold room white
as history.
After a blue dusk
overnight
the windows are so white
one says, "It's not dawn yet."
But it's past dawn;
the olive grove snowed over
and it's still
snowing.

Their bed for the night
was old, the ceiling rafters
tricentenarian.
Two logically
travestied troubadours
(mixing centuries)
met on the road,
sought shelter.
In the farmhouse
attic each lithe boy
discovered (after
wine, after
grappa) the other
had soft
breasts, wet
depths, a traveling

woman's fear-
emboldened heart.

Snow on the olive
groves, snow
falling.
Eight miles
blurred wet road winding
to Florence
they will walk this morning.
On a wooden chair
near the bed,
dark chocolate
in orange foil,
their half-empty
pint of good brandy.

CULTURAL EXCHANGES

—for Catherine Tinker

When Augusta, the teenaged *empleada,*
expressed bewilderment at the two friends'
behavior, "Oh, they're North Americans,"
the *Doña* said, implying that explained
everything. She stretched out, with the telephone
parked on the zipper of her overalls.

Message-pad leaves were scattered over all
the desks and shelves. This house's *empleada*
primarily answered the telephone.
Half the time it was her hometown friends
with city jobs, now, too. "No," she explained,
she wasn't working for Americans

—a single woman. The Americans
wanted her conversations over. All
day they hung around her. (She could have explained
the courtesies owed to an *empleada.*
They were sloppier than her brother's friends!)
In fact, they hung around the telephone.

One of them always had to telephone
someone. She didn't think North Americans
visiting *ought* to have so many friends.
Some afternoons small groups came over, all
middle-class women, with an *empleada*
working at home. They set her down, explained

she could listen, too, while they explained
why women—"Augusta! Get the telephone!"—
were all one class, *Doña* and *empleada*.
They had—"Translate, someone. The Americans . . ."
petitions to circulate over all
the neighborhoods, they hoped she'd show her friends,

to make abortion legal. (Her best friend's
midwife aunt did that, but never explained.)
They showed a film she wished was over. All
that blood! She snuck out, to the telephone
in the study. There, the Americans,
not bickering now, groped and sighed amply. Ada,

her friend, was the group leader's *empleada*.
She telephoned. Could she stay over? All
night? Like the Americans, she explained.

GOING AWAY FROM THE RIVER

Midsummer's Eve: rain slants into docked barges
near the Jardin des Plantes. Cut your losses.

Soon the inhabitants will leave the city
to the international monoglot young.

Out of the smallest, oldest perched village
branch well-marked paths, beside the stream, the ravine.

The streams flow down into the local river.
The footpaths widen into roads back here.

I lived upriver from a different harbor.
Let's say: the boat left without me.

Two altos braided the Drinking Gourd.
Then there was only one voice in the dark.

In October when the fog comes down
early, the moorings are invisible.

Hard to distinguish one old duffel bag,
see the ravine, the rock-path up from dockside.

The highway spared the hill town it bypassed.
I can still get there, leave there, overland.

LA BOUGEOTTE

It's not the name of the next town
or the name of a seasonal wind

though it picks me up like leaves on a windy morning
when T-shirts drying on the line flap "Elsewhere."

It's dark in the kitchen, the refrigerator
hums; no sun on the writing-table.

Walk uphill and look for the Rocher des Fées.
Sit between fields and wait for the Fée des Rochers.

In my orchard, greengages harvested,
the fig tree's second fruit is ripening.

I don't bring food. I eat blackberries
no one else picks. The best ones grow in shade.

The shadow of my own arm and shoulder
over the page protects my eyes from glare.

Even to pee standing up in long grass
is as pleasant as it is necessary.

Creak of the fig tree, chirrup of cicadas:
as if a door had opened, enter craving.

My back's too hot, the flies are insistent.
The fruit made me thirsty. Cold water

and the afternoon shadow of an awning
over a round white table half in the sun:

it's only four miles to Clermont l'Hérault;
not even two of them are on the highway.

LES SERPILLIÈRES

To my upstairs writing-table, to hers downstairs:
crash of the long plank shelf above the stove.

The casserole voided its simmering *poule
au pot,* spending its juices on the tiles.

A jar of capers broke, a jar of curry, a jar of honey.
The kitchen flags reeked: some exotic stew.

She in her loose blue jumper, I in my loose blue shorts
stood, horrified, outside the kitchen doorway,

then she scooped the chicken into the pot;
I dived under the sink for *serpillières:*

squares of soap-roughened cotton fiber, one apiece.
Scouring the corners of our refectory

we gathered honeyed shards of broken glass,
scooped up mounds of capers, herbs and honey.

"Les serpillières! My unlamented marriage!
How he loved to see me on my knees!"

My mother never called them *"serpillières"*
but for hours, after work, she scrubbed floors with them.

"If I'd been alone when that thing came down
I'd have sat on the floor with it and cried!"

"I would have, too—but neither of us were."
One at the lavabo, one at the kitchen basin,

we each washed and wrung a *serpillière*,
hung them on the line outside to dry.

DEAR JOOL, I MISS YOU
IN SAINT-SATURNIN

You mocked me that hot day at Carcassonne,
"We're *tourists* now!" waving the green Michelin.
We'd come to meet your old pals from Tucson—

yards tall, blond, Woolrich-trousered, Aryan.
They wanted dinner well before sunset,
and, sure enough, they were vegetarian,

so I negotiated them an omelette
someplace where we could have our cassoulet.
You'd hiked loved hills with her, as dry and hot

as the Autoroute you drove all day
to bring an old friend and newer one together.
Home was just a postal code away

a village on a hilltop we would rather
the Michelin never noticed. For a while,
home. You came there first with Jean, your mother,

after a voyage meant to reconcile
whom adolescence and divorce divided.
Her white dress plunged to suntanned back, a style

you'd never wear, but picked for her. Your pride did
show, and she mirrored it. I'd been alone,
felt like an orphan, though I tried to hide it.

Then, with my daughter and your mother gone,
you tacked your worksheets to your bedroom walls.
We shaped our hours to work and silence, nun-

like, we thought. Wind chimed matins, and birdcalls
vespers that pealed us to the kitchen where
we cooked our day's rewards. The waterfalls

near Mas Audran were yours, the vineyards were
mine—to walk around. The air was gold
with broom, and grape-leaf, plane-tree green, the air

was blue blue blue July. With wine, we told
each other that we'd be old ladies on
a hill like this, where people still got old

in housedresses and navy cardigans
or patriotic azure *salopettes*.
We'd gossip French and write American.

Our vegetarian compatriates
caught us up on reviews, tenure, careers
and marriages. We smoked French cigarettes

and ordered brandy. They had two more beers.
I stacked ashes around my coffee cup, ill
with sociability. Maverick queer,

maverick straight: two singles to their couple:
I'm sure that the comparison occurred
to both of us. We found the going uphill

worth it, if our hill was the vineyard-
and-orchard-covered slope we'd reascend
laden with *cèpes* and *confit de canard*.

That was three years ago this month. I send
this from one of the wine-veined valley towns
that shone like firefly cages at the end

of day from our roof-terrace. Dusk around
them glowed. We called them "Cities of the Plain"
because it was unsuitable, choked down

our drinks guessing what might be mortal sin
to garrulous hard-working villagers.
We hoped it had to do with doctored wine.

My love is here and mine and I am hers.
Iva is elsewhere, utterly thirteen.
Jean could have told me, "Daughters!" And mothers . . .

This ought to be an elegy for Jean
who came back on last furlough from what grew
in her, from pain, to see you fitted in

the satin gown she wore at twenty-two.
This should be an epithalamion,
but is for solitudes shared in the blue

vat of Meridional air: for you.

LE TRAVAIL RAJEUNIT

Lace cushions were considered by a tall
Martiniquaise;
an Arab housewife (they go out Fridays)
plucked up and measured a divided
skirt. Five cartons, dwarfed by wheeled stalls:

"Everything's to be sold!
Children's clothes? Go through
the boxes. Boy or girl? What size are you
looking for? The paintings I did
myself. I'm eighty-six years old.

I never saw an art school.
Would this fit
your little girl?" "It's exquisite,
but she's too tall." From her slat-sided
barrow, the fruitseller: "You'll

strain your eyes." "It's no strain."
"Do you paint at night?"
The *charcutière* leaned down in her white
stained smock. Glistening forearms collided
with hung hams. Knobbly cane

raised, the painter pushed back her straw hat.
"Never! Mornings

I put a paper block out with the breakfast things.
I set my paints beside it.
I work two hours like that."

Fists in the pockets of her blue
apron, the fruiterer
came round the stand to have a look at her
clipper ships. *"Chouette!* I've never tried it,
but it must be hard to do!"

"Your grandchildren will see them
years from now. 'An eighty-six-
year-old woman, self-taught, from the sticks
of Gignac did these,' they'll say on the guided
tours in the museum!

My grandson's an architect. He's had
bad luck. He's out of work
a year now. Are there jobs in—you're from Belgium?—
New York?
I sell these to help him through." (Why did
they have to be so bad?)

Someone's toddler pushed past my legs
so she could see
one board: Black *abeng*-player under palm tree.
The island woman eyed it
too; then she joined the queue for eggs.

LANGUEDOCIENNE

—for K. J.

This morning the wind came, shaking the quince tree,
making trouble in the chicken yard.

The attic door blew open, windows slammed their case-
ments,
notebooks and envelopes slid off my worktable.

A poplar separating vineyards whispered over
olive and lavender cotton, two shades of summer brown.

Wind makes my head ache. I long for water
surfaces, light on four different riverbanks,

silver trembling on the edge, a waterfall
come up inside me as I come down to you.

Early to the train station; slow bus back through Monday-
shuttered towns;
nectarines under the poplar, wind in the quince tree.

FOR K. J., LEAVING AND COMING BACK

August first: it was a year ago
we drove down from St.-Guilhem-le-Désert
to open up the house in St. Guiraud

rented unseen. I'd stay; you'd go; that's where
our paths diverged. I'd settle down to work,
you'd start the next month of your *Wanderjahr*.

I turned the iron key in the rusted lock
(it came, like a detective-story clue,
in a manila envelope, postmarked

elsewhere, unmarked otherwise) while you
stood behind me in the midday heat.
Somnolent shutters marked our progress. Two

horses grazed on a roof across the street.
You didn't believe me till you turned around.
They were both old, one mottled gray, one white.

Past the kitchen's russet dark, we found
bookshelves on both sides of the fireplace:
Verlaine, *L'Etranger, Notes from the Underground.*

Through an archway, a fresh-plastered staircase
led steeply upward. In a white room stood
a white-clad brass bed. Sunlight in your face

came from the tree-filled window. "You did good."
We laid crisp sheets we would inaugurate
that night, rescued from the *grenier* a wood-

en table we put under the window. Date
our homes from that one, to which you returned
the last week of August, on a late

bus, in shorts, like a crewcut, sunburned
bidasse. Sunburned, in shorts, a new haircut,
with Auden and a racing pulse I'd earned

by "not being sentimental about
you," I sprinted to "La Populaire."
You walked into my arms when you got out.

At a two-minute bus stop, who would care?
"La Populaire" puffed onward to Millau
while we hiked up to the hiatus where

we'd left ourselves when you left St. Guiraud
after an unambiguous decade
of friendship, and some months of something new.

A long week before either of us said
a compromising word acknowledging
what happened every night in the brass bed

and every bird-heralded blue morning
was something we could claim and keep and use;
was, like the house, a place where we could bring

our road-worn, weary selves.

                    Now, we've a pause
in a year we wouldn't have wagered on.
Dusk climbs the tiled roof opposite; the blue's

still sun-soaked; it's a week now since you've gone
to be a daughter in the capital.
(I came north with you as far as Beaune.)

I cook things you don't like. Sometimes I fall
asleep, book open, one A.M., sometimes
I long for you all night in Provençal

or *langue d'oc,* or wish I could, when I'm
too much awake. My early walk, my late
walk mark the day's measures like rhyme.

(There's nothing that I hate—perhaps I hate
the adipose deposits on my thighs
—as much as having to stay put and wait!)

Although a day alone cuts tight or lies
too limp sometimes, I know what I didn't know
a year ago, that makes it the right size:
owned certainty; perpetual surprise.

CELLES

—for Julie Fay

We liked its name: those ones, feminine plural.
We imagined the abandoned village
inhabited by sisters and sororal

friends, restoring walls and foliage.
Each house could have a window on the lake
that now were ruins on the shore: a pillaged

battleground, the site of an earthquake
softened by bushes like a cemetery?
Evacuated by decree, to make

a giant oxbow where there was a valley.
The water licked the town limits and stopped.
The town was saved from drowning, but kept empty.

One evening's rhythms let us interrupt
a drive toward dinner in Lodève, to swerve
down where a gouged raw path made an abrupt

plunge toward water, following the curve
of red clay foothills, Mississippian,
to test your four-wheel drive, or test your nerve,

you said, when we were safely parked. The sun
glare, behind the windshield, gilt the swells
of water. We got out. Your Indian

print dress blew back around you: your hair fell
glowing across your throat. "You ought to be
painted like that, the patron saint of *Celles*

qui vagabondent autour d'une autre vie."
Scrub oak reclaimed what once was the café.
Swallows swooped through what once was the *mairie,*

banked into a thermal, veered halfway
across the water, toward a thicketed
dusk-dappled hill, then back, elegant play

of gliders celebrant above our heads,
spiraling in the current's arabesque.
"If we were the evacuees," you said,

"it wouldn't be so fucking picturesque
to live in Clermont in an HLM.
They were the last ones anybody asked

if making up this place was good for them.
And we are making them up, just as much
as sorceresses flocked here for its name."

We made our way through nascent underbrush
to climb the mayor's ragweed-shattered stairs.
Elbow to elbow, though we didn't touch,

we stood on the wind-littered terrace, where
we watched the sun continue its descent.
We drove away before it disappeared

leaving Those Ones lapped by revenant
shadows, now the cicadas' choral
song broke for nightfall, leaving Celles silent
like us, feminine, plural, transient.

SEPARATE LIVES

The last time I talked to you in my head
was July third, 1986,
in Paris. It was four A.M. A slick
Brazilian singer at Bercy instead
of dinner, last train home. The unmade bed
reproached me, and the lamp I had to fix
whose feeble current threw a ghostly flick-
er up and down the pages as I read,
a contrapuntal subordinate clause
to every sentence. Starting to dogear
my page in *Souvenirs Pieux,* I told
you what and why I thought of Yourcenar,
then blubbered out loud like a six-year-old
"Come home!" although I didn't know where that was.

If you'd gone home, I didn't know where that was
—not uptown, Languedoc, or the Marais
for you, wherever you were. All that day
I'd checked off errands that a person does
at home. Six months before, I'd wept across
just about every street in the *troisième.*
I felt like a surveyor marking them
with snot and tears. Home is where work and loss
intersect until they feel like life.
I lived on that street for as many seasons
as I had lived with you. Nobody's wife
clocked the barges in through harbor grass.
A hard-on has no conscience. Neither has
heartbreak. I didn't want to know your reasons.

Hard break I didn't want: to know your reasons
couldn't have made it easier, or could
it? A good cry beats a rotten mood.
Too good; too bad: she scared herself. Now she's on
her own, third person singular. No *frissons*
transforming verbs whose "thou" is understood.
Half through the night, almost out of the "would
she hear me testifying on my knees on
this not entirely metaphoric floor"
phase, I wasn't wondering who you were
when, why, where, whether we—no, you—were gone
into the winter when the deejays spun
"You have no right / to ask me how I feel."
As if I'd died and lived to tell the tale.

And if I'd died and lived to tell the tale,
recovered from the knowledge I'd recover,
I looked a little less like death warmed over.
Mist fingering the windowpane of pale
dawn wasn't a ghost child tapping "Fail,"
or, if she was, I wasn't frightened of her.
Morning would find me indisposed to suffer
through haunted coffee reading shadow mail:
the letter forwarded two months too late,
the sonnet sequence in a magazine
which wasn't, though it might have been, about
the face on facing page not facing mine,
the Wite-Out in the next-to-the-last line,
the message on your answering machine.

The message on your answering machine
was "Wing it,"—something like "Go, fly, be free."
I chinked my dime through the cacophony
of Twenty-third and Sixth. It played again.
That was the week of leftovers and mean
songs. You'd asked to borrow back your key.
You probably were where you said you'd be.
You probably wouldn't have let me in.
Then Friday night was Sunday afternoon,
the time I didn't know was the last time
you took me in your mouth and made me come,
you took your looseleaf, and a cab downtown.
Now a phone call costs more than a dime.
There were some changes in the interim.

There were some changes in the interim
since you left, since I ran out of tears,
since I ran into you after three years.
The corners of your eyes, behind pale-rimmed
glasses are wet, flood, meltdown. My hands trem-
ble now, yours too. It's cold as hell in here.
The private parts I have behind my ears
fill up when words slow down and handle them,
but I'm too close to home to need a ride.
I don't know if you have the words I need.
I know you didn't need the ones I had.
Would it have come out better than it did
if I had played it on the other side,
if I had shut the book and understood?

If I had shut the book and understood
I'd reached the end of *Souvenirs Pieux*
whose subtext was a dialogue with you
in absentia, and "gone for good"
just the return address when you replied,
I might have grieved for grief. I only knew
I'd finished crying, and there was a blue-
gray hint of day above the slate outside,
a lunch date about seven hours away.
You've brought me back a book, past grief, half known,
still strange, with your name on it, not the one
I wrote, for me to open where you say
things for yourself, that aren't what you said
the last time I talked to you in my head.

DINNER WITH ELIZABETH

"The iron doors opened on a gallery.
Unshaven soldiers in shirtsleeves were playing cards.

There was a light from a few exhausted candles.
Had I seen this before? Was it a painting?

It was nearly four o'clock in the morning.
It occurred to me: this is happening to me."

The wine came. She tasted it, and sent it back,
in a tobacco cloud. She is eighty-four.

"We set up a dormitory for the foundlings
in the ballroom of the borrowed villa.

They took shifts with us on the barricades.
The children who had guns slept with their guns.

We piled the guns in the middle of the ballroom
where they could all see them. Then they could all sleep.

Can you find your way back home from here?"
She left Vermont for Paris fifty years,

four wars ago. I am a Bronx Jew
whose leasehold names me resident for two.

DAYS OF 1944: THREE FRIENDS

—for Odile Hellier and Geneviève Pastre

I

"It wasn't safe to stay in Saint-Brieuc,
Mother took us across the gash in France,
the rift between *langue d'oïl* and *langue d'oc,*
between the Occupation and Pétain's

lackeys. Her uncle lived near Montpellier.
For a while, my father had good luck.
When he appeared on my second birthday,
we all ate cherries as if they were cake.

Nine months later, my brother was born.
Then she had three babies on her hands.
My father's letters came, were passed round, torn
and burned. Spies found the Breton Résistance

or bought someone, nobody can be sure.
My father and my grandmother were shot.
The Germans burned our house. The furniture
was parceled out at auction, lot by lot."

II

"We had to walk from Rodez to Millau.
My sister, with her patent-leather shoes
tied to a string, sat, cried, and wouldn't go
further. I was ten. I walked, I knew,

I thought, what it was like to want to die
when we stopped. People waited in the Gare
where no more trains went. I found one bench I
stretched out on. 'I don't care,' I said, 'we are

hungry already.' When my cousin came,
my mother had to hit me to dislodge
me. Only one more mile. The rain
gave the stiff winter houses camouflage

uniforms. I followed the cousin, numb
as a stone. My sister's shoes shone, two
crystals. I'd left my fossil box at home.
But that was nothing. Just what we lived through."

III

"I was a walking baby in the Bronx.
My astigmatic father was 4-F.
Mother saved bacon grease in coffee-cans
for ration points. She was an orphan—*trefe*

and kosher didn't matter. We were Jews
I knew, before I tried to learn to read—
and that we lived on Eastburn Avenue,
and that you grew a baby from a seed.

My father's mother's older sister's son
was a pilot, shot down over some
place across the ocean with an un-
familiar vowel. Near where she came from.

I saw his picture. In his peaked hat he
looked like the soldiers on the magazine
covers. I only knew a Nazi
was bad. I didn't know, if I had been

born who I was, *there* . . . They said no one knew.
I know the countries, not the counties or
towns my grandparents left—whose other Jews
the fire took, while you lived, I played, at war."

FOR JEAN MIGRENNE

Mauve into purple, bent on foam-green stems,
a bank of lavender washed by the rain
recalls Languedoc, though this is on the plain
of Caen, between two blocks of HLMs.
Down south, the hedge around the one *lycée*
is rosemary, high as a young girl's eyes.
Here, notebooks bloat in puddles on the grass:
school's out, and has been out for seven days.
Cahiers au feu, le maître au milieu!
My friend's an English teacher, but he knows
more about setting words on fire than those
bookburning kids gone summer-savage do.
Man, woman, *gouine* and *pédé,* Jew, white and black:
our language is annealed, transmuted, changed
out of our many, into his mother tongue
that will be ours because he brought us back,
faithful, into the words he earned with need.
His uncles followed herds and farmed the rocks
for earth-apples, drank hard. There were no books.
The scrubbed boy went to school and learned to read.
He learned to read the rocks that, aeons old,
have lives inscribed in layers beneath the schist.
He learned how to become an alchemist
who turns the New World's ore to Gallic gold.
Metaphor the solvent, words dissolve
and crystallize again in the alembic.
Alexandrine clusters replace iambic
pentameters; crystals of ten-turned-twelve

glow, faceted, in readers' eyes, where I've
seen my own sea-changed lines catch light. As if
the words acknowledged him for their new life
they lead him back into their other lives:
Josephine Baker's black gold in the sleaze
light of a nightclub for expatriates,
heroin dawns in Lower East Side squats,
revival-tent hot nights in Mississippi's
swamp country, cities of the dead in Queens,
kosher food, soul food, the Black Bourgeoisie
whose son, running, with blameless grocery
bags, home, is shot by cops. He was sixteen.
The translator haunts him in rituals
performed by cliques in lunchrooms and study halls,
the semiology of toilet stalls.
The translator transforms someone's first menses,
first neutral pronouns and conditional tenses,
first systematic derangement of the senses.
He feels his way along a knot of words
tangled with anger, music, grief, love, play.
Some local teenaged daredevil has spray-
painted *Je T'Aime* on a peeling billboard's
Fiat—no proper name, so no dispute—
where we retrace our path, carrying bread
for lunch, and argue meters as we head
across the road that feeds the Autoroute.

GOING BACK TO THE RIVER

—for K. J.

Dusk, iridescent gasoline floats on the
rain-puddles, peacock feathers on macadam.
  Schoolgirl beneath an awning pulls her
  collar up, here comes her bus. She's gone now.

Nine-thirty, and there's light behind thunderheads.
Storm over, in an hour it will rain again.
  Meal done, across the street a neighbor
  shakes out her tablecloth from the window.

I have a reading lamp and an open book.
Last glass of wine, last morsel of Saint-André
  prolong my dinner and my chapter
  into the ten o'clock Haydn program.

What will I say to you when I write to you?
(What would I say to someone who isn't you?)
  I'm home, I've cleaned the kitchen, taken
  charge of my solitude, taken long baths.

What do I tell myself when I open and
write in the notebook keeping me company?
  Don't stay indoors tomorrow morning.
  Do the week's shopping at Sunday market.

Go to the river, take what it offers you.
When you were young, it guarded and promised you
  that you would follow other rivers
  oceans away from a landlocked childhood.

Yes, I indulge myself in hyperbole
since I'm not going out for a walk in this
     wet weather, though I'd walk from someone
     else's place, stop on the bridge, look over.

Seine, Thames and Hudson (sounds like a publisher):
one river flows down into another one.
     Where did I sit and read alone, who
     walked with me which afternoon, which evening?

There was a river when I was leaving you.
That morning, with our *café con leche,* we
     slouched on a bench above the Hudson,
     washed in the wind of a near departure.

Not rupture: each one went where she had to go.
Still, I'd be hours and borders away from you.
     We bluffed like adolescent soldiers
     at the significant bridge or crossroad.

"Your father," you said, "would have been proud of you."
"My mother never would have imagined it."
     Poor Jews in an antagonistic
     city, they pulled in their walls around them.

One city would have looked like another one:
hard work, a clean house, food without seasoning.
     Scrub Europe from a neutral palate,
     blend and assimilate, mistrust strangers,

know in an instant which are the *lanzmänner*.
No Yiddish pet names, gossip or baby talk.
   Brownshirts outside the door would pass on
   innocent, bland Mid-Atlantic Standard.

Is any accent that safely nondescript?
Their child, I bruise my brain on two languages
   (neither the one they lost) four decades
   after they earned me this freedom, passing

as what they weren't: rooted American.
Their daughter, I come home to two continents,
   live with my roots tied up in parcels,
   still impecunious, maybe foolish.

Another child of children of immigrants
(Russian, Italian), you've chosen languages
   written in symbols meant to have no
   country of origin, color, gender

(though every symbol's chiseled with history).
There, you are learning chemical formulae:
   meals on the run, a book you started
   months ago under the bed, abandoned.

Life's not forever, love is precarious.
Wherever I live, let me come home to you
   as you are, I as I am, where you
   meet me and walk with me to the river.

AGAINST SILENCE

AGAINST SILENCE

—for Margaret Delany

Because you are
my only daughter's only grandmother,
because your only grandchild is my child
I would have wished you to be reconciled

to how and what
I live. No name frames our connection, not
"in-laws." I hoped, more than "your son's ex-wife."
I've known you now for two-thirds of my life.

You had good friends,
good books, good food, good manners, a good mind.
I was fifteen. I wished this were my home.
(None of my Jewish aunts read *I. F. Stone's*

Weekly, or shopped at Saks
Fifth Avenue, none of them grew up Black
working poor, unduped and civilized.)
I know you were unpleasantly surprised

when, eighteen, we
presented you with the *fait accompli*
of courthouse marriage in one of two states
where no age-of-consent or miscegenat-

ion laws applied.
Your sister's Beetle—bumps knife-thrusts inside
after a midnight Bellevue D and C—
brought me uptown. You took care of me,

a vomit-green
white girl in your son's room. Had I been
pregnant? Aborted? No. Miscarried? Yes.
You didn't ask. I didn't tell, just guessed

what you knew. You
asked my mother to lunch. I'd "had the flu."
She greeted me, "Your hair looks like dog shit.
Cut it or do something to it!"

I burned with shame
you saw what kind of family I came
from. Could you imagine me more
than an unacceptable daughter-in-law?

When, fortified,
I went home to the Lower East Side,
my new job, art school at night and my queer
marriage, you were, understatedly, there.

For a decade's
holidays, there was always a place
set for me, if I was in New York.
Your gifts groomed me: a dark-green wool for work,

pin-striped Villager
shirts. I brought books, wine, an Irish mohair
shawl laced with velvet ribbons. I came back
from London with a kangaroo-pouch pack

containing your
exuberant golden granddaughter.
You never asked me why I lived alone
after that. Feast-day invitations

stopped—Iva went
with her father. Evenings you spent
with friends, but normal Sundays you'd be in.
I'd call, we'd come a little before noon.

Because you did
that, Sundays there'd be fried liver or shad
roe, or bacon, hot rolls, hash, poached eggs.
We ate while Iva tugged around our legs

the big plush bear
you gave her. From the pile beside your chair
I picked over, passed you the book reviews
in exchange for White Sales and the *News*

of the Week in
Review. Your mother, ninety-eight, deep in
somnolent cushions, eighty years' baker of rolls,
wakened by child-noise, called the child, and told

her stories
nine decades vivid, liking the rose-gold three-
year-old, British born, Black by law
and choice as she was, with diaspora

Virginia, Harlem;
linking me, listening beside them
with you. She died at one hundred and two
and I, childlike, took it for granted you

would certainly
be bad-mouthing Republicans with me
for two more decades' editorial page.
Seventy-four was merely middle age.

The question some
structuralist with me on a podium,
exalted past politeness, called *"idiote"*
(a schoolyard-brawl word) "For whom do you write?"

I could have answered
(although it wouldn't have occurred
to anyone to ask it after that),
"I write for somebody like Margaret"

—but I'd written
names for acts and actors which, by then,
reader, you'd read, and read me out, abhorred
in print lives you'd let live behind closed doors.

You wouldn't be
in that debate, agree to disagree.
We would need time, I thought. This can resume,
like any talk, with fresh air in the room

and a fresh pot
of coffee, in the fall. But it will not.
Some overload blocked silence in your brain.
A starched girl starts your syllables again.

You held your tongue
often enough to hear, when you were young,
and older, more than you wanted to discuss.
Some things were more acceptable, nameless.

You sometimes say
names amidst the glossolalial
paragraphs that you enunciate
now, unanswerable as, "Too late."

Baffled between
intention and expression, when your son
says, "Squeeze my hand, once for 'no,' twice for 'yes,' "
you squeeze ten times, or none, gratuitous.

A hemisphere
away from understanding where you are,
mourning your lost words, I am at a loss
for words to name what my loss of you is,
what it will be, or even what it was.

About the Author

Marilyn Hacker is the author of six books of poetry, including the verse novel *Love, Death, and the Changing of the Seasons* (1986), and *Presentation Piece,* which received the National Book Award in 1975 and was a Lamont Poetry Selection of the Academy of American Poets. Her criticism and reviews appear in *Grand Street, The Nation,* and *The Women's Review of Books.*

Born in the Bronx on Thanksgiving Day, 1942, she now lives in Manhattan and in Paris.